Sugar Inspirations

Wild Flowers

On Top of the World's Best Selling Cakes

Dedication

This book is dedicated with love to my grandfather, Ernest Blair,
and to the memory of my grandmothers,
Margaret Blair and Florence Dunn.

First published 1995 by Merehurst Limited.
This edition printed 2003 for Culpitt Limited.
Reprinted 2005

Merehurst is an imprint of Murdoch Books® UK Ltd

Copyright © Merehurst Limited 1995
ISBN 1-85391-413-4

A catalogue record of this book is available from the British Library.

Editor: Helen Southall
Design: Anita Ruddell
Photographer: Sue Atkinson

Colour separation by P & W Graphics Pty Ltd. Singapore
Printed in China

Contents

Introduction

Wild flowers of the countryside make wonderful subjects for sugarcraft. Their natural beauty of colour and shape will enhance any celebration cake.

I have always had an interest in flowers but since starting to decorate cakes over eight years ago, my love for them has grown. I now regularly spend some of my spare time, either by myself or on separate occasions with my friends Alice, Stephanie and Tombi, walking through the countryside or visiting flower shops, botanical gardens and garden centres in search of something different! We had several fun days trying to find the flowers to copy for this book! I now have mental pictures of the places where we found the plants so that next time I need a flower I will know where to look. It is a good idea to take a pencil and note pad with you on your hunt for wild flowers so you can write about and draw the various parts of the flowers you find. Some flowers can be picked, as long as you don't damage the plant itself, but many species of wild flower are endangered and should only be looked at!

Sometimes, when making sugar flowers, a little artistic licence is needed, creating the character of a plant or flower instead of striving for botanical correctness. I also find that if the work is too neat and accurate, it can look lifeless and lack soul. Real flowers in sprays and bouquets don't last very well without water; with sugar work there are very few boundaries, so have fun!

Equipment

To make the flowers and cake designs in this book, you will need the following standard equipment. Details of other items needed to make individual flowers are given with each set of instructions. All the equipment is available from specialist cake-decorating suppliers.

Board and rolling pin
A non-stick rolling board and pin make it much easier to roll out paste without sticking. Grooved boards and pins are available; these are very useful for creating ridges on petals and leaves to allow them to be individually wired. I have made grooves in the back of my non-stick board. To do this yourself, heat a metal skewer until it turns red hot, and then brand the board several times until the depth of groove needed is achieved. (I have a few different depths and lengths on mine.) Scrape off the excess plastic. Smooth the board by rubbing with some fine glass paper.

Mexican hat board
This board has holes in it of various depths and sizes. To use it, start off with the paste quite thick, and roll it out over the required hole, until the surface paste is thin enough. Remove the paste from the board and you will be left with a thick area in the centre. This forms the back of a flower or calyx.

Modelling tools
Celsticks are useful for rolling out, for softening and cupping petals, and also for hollowing out the centres of flowers. A bone-end tool can also be used to soften edges and cup petals on smaller flowers and foliage. My favourite tool is the dresden, which can be used for veining and hollowing, and to create serrated/frilly edges on leaves and flowers.

Cutters
I tend to use these to cut out basic shapes – they save time and allow consistency of size and shape of flowers. There are many different types available on the market.

Veiners
I use mainly commercially made double-sided veiners that have

been made from an impression of a real flower or leaf.

Pads

These are used to hold the paste while you are softening or veining a petal or leaf. You can also work on the palm of your hand, but this can be tiring and the paste often sticks.

Paintbrushes

I like to use 5mm (¼ inch) wide sable/synthetic blend brushes. These are soft but firm at the same time. Rounded brushes are difficult to control and often colour very unevenly. Finer paintbrushes are also needed for painting details and dusting small areas.

Tape shredder

This is used to cut floristry tape into various widths. You will need to replace the blades from time to time.

Colouring

Paste and powder food colourings work best. They can both be used for colouring the paste before you make a flower and can be mixed with either water or clear alcohol (such as vodka) to paint markings on petals afterwards. To achieve authentic colours, it is best to work with flower paste that is a lot paler than the finished flower should be, and to dust the flower a darker colour once it is made. Try to experiment with your colouring, mixing colours to achieve the effect that is required. For very pale work, you can add either cornflour or white petal dust (blossom tint) before you start colouring the flower. There are a few mixtures that I use frequently:

Dark green

This is very good if you want to add depth to a leaf. Mix one part jade with one part moss, and then darken with black and nutkin. I use different mixtures of various tones.

Burgundy

Mix two parts plum with one part each of red, cornflower blue and nutkin brown. Add a half part of black.

Purple/blue

Purple and blue mixtures are used frequently in wild-flower-making. To give slightly different effects, I mix cornflower blue with either violet, plum, fuchsia or red. Another favourite of mine is a very soft powder blue which is achieved by mixing equal quantities of lavender and bluebell.

Glazing

There are many ways to glaze sugar petals and leaves. The steaming method does not give a permanent glaze but improves the 'dusty' appearance of finished flowers or leaves that don't need a shiny surface. Hold each leaf or petal in the steam from a boiling kettle for a few seconds, until it turns slightly shiny. Take great care as too much steam can soften and dissolve the sugar.

For a more permanent and effective glaze, use confectioner's varnish. Used neat (full glaze), this gives a very high gloss, which is ideal for berries, but for leaves, dilute the varnish with iso-propyl alcohol (available from chemists). Place the varnish and alcohol in a lidded container and shake to mix. The glaze can be used straight away. Dip the leaves or petals, one at a time, into the glaze, shake off the excess and dry on absorbent kitchen paper. The glaze can be applied with a paintbrush, but I find the brush strokes tend to remove the petal dust. The following glazes are used in this book.

¼ glaze

Three-quarters alcohol to quarter part varnish. This is useful for leaves that don't have much shine; the glaze just takes away the flat, dusty look of a leaf.

½ glaze

Equal proportions of alcohol and varnish. This gives the leaf a very natural shine and is useful for rose leaves.

¾ glaze

Quarter part alcohol to three-quarters varnish. This gives a semi-gloss.

Flower paste

I usually buy flower paste ready made up as it is more consistent than home-made paste, and because I like a paste that is quite soft and that stretches very well. The paste that I buy can be worked on for quite a while before it starts to dry out. However, you can make your own from the following:

5 teaspoons cold water
2 teaspoons powdered gelatine
500g (1lb) icing (confectioner's) sugar, sifted
3 teaspoons gum tragacanth
2 teaspoons liquid glucose
3 teaspoons white vegetable fat or 2 teaspoons soya oil
1 egg white (size 2)

1 Mix the cold water and gelatine together in a small heatproof bowl and leave to stand for 30 minutes. Sift the icing sugar and gum tragacanth into the bowl of a heavy-duty mixer and fix the bowl to the machine.

2 Place the bowl with the gelatine mixture over a saucepan of hot water and stir until the gelatine has dissolved. Warm a teaspoon in hot water and then measure out the liquid glucose (the heat should help ease the glucose off the spoon). Add the glucose and white fat or soya oil to the gelatine, and continue to heat until the ingredients are all dissolved and thoroughly mixed.

3 Add the dissolved mixture to the icing sugar with the egg white. Fix the beater to the machine and turn the mixer on to its lowest speed. Beat until all the ingredients are mixed, then increase the speed to maximum until the paste is white and stringy.

4 Remove the paste from the bowl and rub a thin layer of white fat over it (to prevent the outer part drying out).Place in a plastic bag and store in an airtight container. Allow the paste to rest and mature for at least 12 hours before using it.

Lords and Ladies

During the spring this attractive and unusual plant has a decorative green sheath gradually dying away to reveal green then orange berries.

Materials

18, 20, 24 and 30-gauge wires
Pale and mid-green, melon and
nasturtium flower paste
(see page 6)
Violet, cornflower blue, nutkin,
black, primrose, moss, dark
green, skintone, lemon, tangerine, red and cream petal dust
(blossom tint)
¾ glaze and full glaze
(see page 6)

Equipment

White and pale green floristry
tape
Lords and ladies cutters (604)
Scalpel
Absorbent kitchen paper
Lords and ladies leaf veiner

Spadix

1 Tape over a half length of 18-gauge wire with pale green floristry tape, and moisten the end with egg white. Take a medium ball of white or pale green paste, insert the wire and work quickly between your fingers and thumb to cover about 7.5cm (3 inches) of the wire. The lower half of the spadix should be slightly thinner. Attach another ball of paste to the base of the spadix to give the base a little padding.

2 To make the pollen, mix together equal propor-
tions of violet and cornflower blue petal dust with a little black, skintone and nutkin added. Moisten the spadix with egg white and roll in the pollen colour. Allow to dry.

Spathe

3 Roll out some pale green paste (not too finely).
Place the lords and ladies cutter on the paste and cut out the spathe. Place the paste on a

pad, and soften the edges and hollow out the lower part of the paste using a large celstick.

4 Draw the broad end of a dresden tool down the inside of both edges to give a slightly curled edge. Next, using the fine end of the dresden tool, mark a series of fine veins fol-lowing the curve of the spathe, to cover the whole surface.

5 Moisten the base of the spathe and place the spadix on the right-hand side.

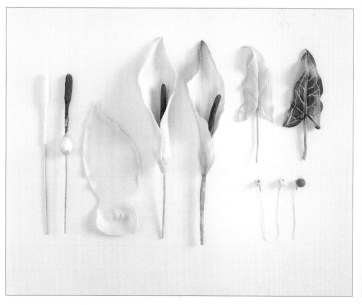

Gently roll the two together, being very careful not to get pollen on the paste. Pinch the tip of the spathe to form a fine point, then hang upside-down until it is firm enough to handle. Rearrange the edge until you are happy with it.

6 Using a mixture of primrose and moss green, dust the edges, the base and a little inside the spathe very lightly. Dust the edges with skintone, aubergine and the violet/cornflower blue pollen mixture. Steam slightly to glaze (see page 6).

7 To thicken the stem, cut some kitchen paper into strips and wrap around the wire, taping over the top with ½-width green floristry tape. Dust with skintone and moss green.

Leaves

8 Lords and ladies leaves are usually plain or dark spotted green, but I prefer to use the leaves from a similar species that has pale veins.

9 Tape over a 20-gauge wire with ½-width green tape, leaving about 4 cm (1½ inches) of wire uncovered at one end. You will need to repeat this about five times to add bulk to each wire.

10 Roll out some mid-green paste using a grooved rolling pin or on a grooved board. Cut out a leaf. Insert the moistened wire, place the leaf into the veiner, and press the two sides together. Remove, place on a pad and soften the edges. Allow to dry slightly.

11 Dust the leaf with dark green and moss green petal dust. Allow to dry completely and then dip into a ¾ glaze. Allow to dry, then if you wish you can scratch away the veins using a scalpel.

Berries

12 Cut a 30-gauge wire into five, hook the end of each and moisten. Using the green, melon and nasturtium-coloured pastes, roll lots of small balls, using the orange paste to make slightly larger berries. Pull a hooked wire into each ball, leaving the hook showing through. Using a scalpel, create indents around the hook. Allow to dry.

13 Cover a piece of 20-gauge wire with white floristry tape and then start to tape in the berries (in no particular order). Dust the berries with lemon, tangerine and red petal dust, adding a little moss to finish. Glaze a few times with full glaze. Thicken the stem as before with kitchen paper.

14 The bract at the base of the berries is the dead flower. To make this, use white floristry tape dusted with cream and nutkin petal dust. Using a scalpel, draw veins on the tape and then cut into the edge to make it ragged.

Note

Remember the flowers and fruit would not be growing side by side, so use them separately.

Wood Crane's-Bill

This true Geranium can vary quite a lot in colour, from reddish-purple to pinkish-lilac to more of a blue! It grows in woodlands, hedgebanks and meadows.

Materials

24, 26, 28 and 30-gauge wires
Aubergine, plum, violet, corn-flower blue, dark green and holly/ivy petal dust (blossom tint)
Fine white stamens
Pale pink and mid-holly/ivy flower paste (see page 6)
White spirit
¼ glaze (see page 6)

Equipment

Pale green and white floristry tape
Blossom cutter (F9)
Calyx cutter (R13A)
Scalpel
Japanese maple leaf cutters (JM1–3)
Crane's-bill leaf veiners

Pistil and stamens

1 Cut a piece of 26-gauge wire in two. Using a short piece of ¼-width white floristry tape, tape the end of the wire, leaving a tiny flap at the end. Cut this flap into five very fine strands. Dust with a little plum petal dust.

2 Paint the tips of five fine stamens (both ends) with a little aubergine petal dust

mixed with white spirit. Bend in half to form ten and tape slightly below the pistil.

Flower

3 Roll out some pink paste, leaving the centre slightly thicker (a Mexican hat board, see page 4, is helpful here). Cut out a flower using the blossom cutter. Place the flower on a pad, and use a celstick to soften the edges and slightly stretch each petal.

4 Place the flower back on the board and, using the fine end of a dresden tool, draw some fine veins on each petal, trying not to press too hard to avoid tearing the paste.

5 Roll out some green paste fairly thinly and cut out a shape with the calyx cutter. Place on the pad and soften the edges. Draw the fine end of the dresden tool down the centre of each sepal to make a central vein.

6 Moisten the inside of the calyx and position the flower on top (you should be

able to see a sepal in between each of the petals). Thread the stamens through the centre of the flower, pinching the back firmly when you reach the top of the stem, a little below the stamens. Allow to dry for about 1 hour before dusting with plum, starting at the edge and working towards the centre (which should be left pale). Add a little violet/cornflower blue mix to the edges. Allow the flower to dry thoroughly.

7 If you're feeling brave, use a scalpel to scratch away some very fine pale veins on each petal.

Half flowers and buds

8 Make half-open flowers as above, but close the petals a little more. For buds, attach small balls of green paste to the ends of hooked 30-gauge wires. Pinch a tiny point at the tip and mark five indents with a scalpel to form the sepals. Make several buds in various sizes.

9 To make a larger bud, attach a slightly larger ball of paste to a 28-gauge wire. Roll out some more green paste and cut a calyx. Work the edges and vein as before, moisten and stick around the ball.

Leaves

10 Roll out some green paste fairly thickly using either a grooved rolling pin or board. Cut out the leaves using the Japanese maple cutters. Insert a 26-gauge wire into each leaf. Place it back on the board and use a celstick to broaden each section of the leaf. Vein using the crane's-bill veiners. To create the jagged edge, you can either use a scalpel or fine scissors to cut out V shapes, or, for speed, you can use the broad end of the dresden tool, pressing it against the edge of the leaf on to the board. Allow to firm slightly.

11 Dust a little plum on the edges of each leaf, dark green from the centre to the edge, and then holly/ivy on top. Glaze using the ¼ glaze.

Assembly

12 Tape the buds and flowers together in clumps, attaching some small strands of cut floristry tape at each junction. Join together various clumps, adding the leaves in pairs, either side of the large junctions. Keep on adding until you have formed a good display. As the plant gets larger you might find that taping each large clump on to several 24-gauge wires gives a little more support.

13 Dust the stems with plum and then with the various green petal dusts, as for the leaves.

Ramsons

Otherwise known as wild garlic, you can usually smell this attractive plant long before you see it!

Materials

24 and 30-gauge wires
White and green flower paste
(see page 6)
Fine white stamens
Lemon, moss, primrose, dark green and cream petal dust
(blossom tint)
½ glaze (see page 6)

Equipment

Scalpel
Pale green floristry tape
Pointed six-petal cutter (N6)
Fine wire
Leaf texture tool

Ovary and stamens

1 Hook and moisten a 30-gauge wire and attach a tiny ball of pale green paste to the hooked end. Using a scalpel, divide this into three sections. Cut a short piece of stamen and stick it into the centre.

2 Take three stamens, bend in half to form six, and tape tightly behind the ovary using ¼-width floristry tape. Dust the tips with lemon petal dust and lightly colour the ovary with primrose and moss green.

Flower

3 Roll out a small piece of white paste thinly, leaving it slightly thicker in the middle (a Mexican hat board, see page 4, can speed this up, if you use one of the smaller holes). Cut out the petals using the six-petal cutter. Place the paste on a pad, soften the edges with a celstick, and then vein each petal with the broad end of a dresden tool.

4 Moisten the centre of the petals, pull the stamens through and give the back of the flower a good pinch, to make sure it is secure. Pinch the tip of each petal slightly between your finger and thumb. Allow to dry, and then dust the back lightly with a little moss green.

Buds

5 The buds are quite small and cone-shaped. Attach a cone of white paste to the end of a hooked, moistened 30-gauge wire. The easiest way to mark the petals is to make a 'cage'. You will need six short pieces of fine wire, taped together at the base. Open the wires and insert the bud (tip first), close the wires and squeeze. Release the wire and twist the bud slightly.

Leaves

6 Roll out some green flower paste using a grooved board or rolling pin. Cut out the leaf shape using a scalpel. Insert a 24-gauge wire and use a leaf texture tool to vein the length of the leaf. Mark a central vein with the fine end of the dresden tool, and then soften the edges slightly. Allow to dry over a slight curve.

Assembly

7 The buds and flowers all come out at the same point and there are two bracts at the base of this. Use two pieces of floristry tape, cut a point at one end of each and vein using the dresden tool. Dust with a little cream and moss, and tape at the base of the flowers.

Speedwell

There are over twenty species of speedwell in the British Isles, this flower is modelled on germander speedwell.

Materials

White and spruce flower paste
(see page 6)
30 and 33-gauge wires
Fine white stamens
Bluebell, lavender, violet, cornflower blue, white, dark green,
holly/ivy and plum petal dust
(blossom tint)
White spirit
¼ glaze (see page 6)

Equipment

Scalpel or fine scissors
Tiny daphne cutter (466)
Small rose petal cutters
Nettle veiner
Pale green floristry tape

Buds

1 These are tiny cone-shaped pieces of white flower paste attached to the ends of 30-gauge wires. Mark four indents on each bud using a scalpel or scissors.

2 Roll out some spruce paste and cut out a tiny calyx for each bud. (To make a tiny calyx cutter, squeeze together the petals on one side of the daphne cutter with a pair of fine pliers.) Soften each sepal with a celstick and mark a cen-tre vein with a dresden tool. Moisten and attach to the bud.

Flower

3 Roll out a tiny piece of white paste, leaving the centre slightly thicker. Cut out flower shapes using the daphne cutter. Broaden three of the petals with a small celstick or cocktail stick (toothpick). Open the centre of the flower with a cocktail stick. Roll a tiny ball of paste and stick it into the centre using the point of the cocktail stick.

4 Thread a moistened, hooked, 33-gauge wire through the centre of the flower. Pinch the back firmly to make sure it is secure. Insert two short stamens into the centre, one either side of the main petal. A third stamen can be added to represent the pistil. Allow to dry slightly.

5 Dust the flower with equal proportions of bluebell/lavender, and then darken the edges slightly using violet and cornflower blue. Try to avoid dusting the centre, as this should be bright white. (If you do cover the centre, you can paint over the top using a little white petal dust.)

6 Mix a little white spirit with cornflower blue and violet petal dust and paint very fine lines on each petal, radiating from the centre.

7 Make a tiny calyx for each flower, as in step 2, and add to the back of the flower, positioning it so that each sepal is between two petals.

Leaves

8 Roll out some spruce paste on a very fine-grooved board. Cut out the leaves using small rose petal cutters, remembering that the leaves tend to grow in pairs of the same size. Insert a moist-ened 33-gauge wire into at least half the length of each leaf. Vein using the nettle veiner.

9 The edges of the leaves are very finely scalloped. To do this cut the edge with a fine pair of scissors. Dust the leaves with holly/ivy and dark green dust. Glaze with ¼ glaze.

Assembly

10 Tape the buds together first, then add the flowers and then the leaves in pairs. Dust the stems with plum and holly/ivy.

Spring Woodland Cake

I designed this cake for my friend Maria's birthday, but I didn't finish it in time! She has since forgiven me! I've included a selection of flowers that I observed last spring during one of my Sunday-afternoon walks.

Materials

25cm (10 inch) teardrop cake
Apricot glaze
1.5kg (3lb) almond paste (marzipan)
Clear alcohol (kirsch or vodka)
2kg (4lb) ivory sugarpaste (ready-to-roll icing)
Royal icing
Pink, pale green and black paste food colourings
Plum, lavender, bluebell, holly/ivy, dark green, cream, tangerine, nutkin, black, apricot and aubergine petal dust (blossom tint)
¼ glaze (see page 6)
Flower paste (see page 6)
Sugarpaste (ready-to-roll icing)

Equipment

Sugarpaste smoothers
36cm (14 inch) oval cake board
Greaseproof paper (parchment)
piping bags
Nos. 1 and 0 piping tubes (tips)
Scriber
Nos. 1 and 2 paintbrushes
Two thin pieces of cake card
Staysoft flower base
Confectioner's varnish

Flowers

2 lords and ladies flowers and 9 leaves (see page 7)
4 ramson stems (see page 11)
6 wood crane's-bill stems (see page 9)
5 speedwell stems (see page 12)

Preparation

1 Brush the cake with apricot glaze and cover with almond paste. Leave to dry. Moisten the cake with alcohol and cover with sugarpaste, using the smoothers to achieve a good finish. Allow to dry.

2 Cover the board with sugarpaste and position the cake on top. Pipe a snail's-trail around the bottom edge of the cake using ivory royal icing in a paper piping bag fitted with a no. 1 tube.

Brush embroidery

3 Trace the floral design on page 46 on to a piece of greaseproof paper and scribe in sections on to the cake. Repeat as many times as required to fill the top edge of the cake to your taste.

4 Colour some royal icing pink and pale green. Fill a piping bag fitted with a no. 1 tube with the green icing, and use to outline a leaf. Using the largest paintbrush that the design will take, moisten with water and brush the icing from the edge to the central vein. It should form veins on the leaf.

5 Fill another bag with the pink icing and outline a petal at a time on the crane's-bill flowers. Moisten the brush and make strong, long strokes down the petal. Repeat to complete the flower. Pipe ten tiny dots in the flower centre, using some white royal icing in another piping bag fitted with a no. 0 tube. Fill in the smaller flowers using this icing and a smaller brush.

6 When the design is finished, you can add definition by painting on top of the flowers using the various petal dusts mixed with a little alcohol.

Arrangements

7 The flowers are arranged in staysoft (an inedible florist's material). To protect the

cake, place the staysoft on a piece of thin cake card before placing on the cake board. The staysoft can also be covered with green sugarpaste before arranging the flowers.

8 Place the large flowers in first and fill in the gaps with the smaller flowers and foliage. Arrange some dead leaves at the base of the arrangements. These are made from cream flower paste, veined and softened, and then dusted with different combinations of cream, tangerine, nutkin brown and black petal dusts. Glaze using a ¼ glaze.

Mouse

9 This is modelled using a mixture of equal proportions of sugarpaste and flower paste. The fur has been created by mixing the two pastes together to form a very sticky paste. This is spread on to the mouse and then textured with a

scriber. Allow to dry slightly and then dust the mouse with cream, nutkin and a little black petal dust, leaving the chin and chest white. Dust the ears and nose with a little apricot petal dust. The eyes are glazed with a mixture of confectioner's varnish and black paste colouring.

Arrangement

It seems to me that some of the rules of commercial flower arranging and floristry are made to be broken! Remember that beauty is always in the eye of the beholder. Arranging flowers in either florist's staysoft or oasis can help the sugercrafter to achieve large and dramatic effects that would be more difficult if a sugar medium were used. You must, however, make sure that these inedible materials do not come into contact with the cake's surface. Place the staysoft on either a thin cake card or a piece of perspex before

placing it on the cake or board. The staysoft can be covered with green sugarpaste if wished.

Materials

3 lords and ladies flowers (see page 7)
1 large and several small wood crane's-bill stems (see page 9)
3 ramson stems (see page 11)
3 speedwell stems (see page 12)
Lords and ladies leaves and other foliage

Equipment

Staysoft flower base
Small cake card
Non-toxic glue
Fine pliers
Wire cutters

1 Fix the staysoft to the cake card with a small amount of non-toxic glue.

2 Arrange the three lords and ladies in the staysoft at different heights and facing in slightly different directions.

3 Place the large crane's-bill stem behind the main flowers and some of the smaller stems at the sides. Add the ramsons at different heights and then fill with speedwell and foliage.

White Waterlily

Although called 'white' waterlily, this flower has a gentle pink tinge to the outer petals. It's the largest of the native wild flowers, measuring a maximum of 20cm (8 inches) in diameter!

Materials

18, 20, 26 and 28-gauge wires
Lemon, white and mid-green flower paste (see page 6)
Lemon, moss, primrose, plum, pink, dark green and holly/ivy petal dust (blossom tint)
½ glaze and full glaze (see page 6)
Mimosa-coloured pollen dust
Cornflour

Equipment

White and green floristry tape
Six-petal daisy cutter (N6)
Cattleya orchid wing petal cutters (3, 6, 9, 12)
Amaryllis veiner (or any other fine veiner)
Fine pliers
Very large nasturtium leaf veiners
Scalpel

Stamens

1 Tape over a piece of 20-gauge wire with white floristry tape, and bend an open hook at one end. Moisten the hook and attach a ball of lemon paste. Hollow out the top slightly and allow to dry.

2 Roll out some lemon paste and cut out two six-petal daisy shapes. Soften the edges with a celstick and mark a central vein on each petal with a dresden tool. Stick the two shapes together and then thread on to the wired shape. Curl the stamens into the centre. Dust the stamens with lemon petal dust and, as the centre has a wet look, paint the very centre with full glaze.

3 The outer stamens are made by twisting ½-width white floristry tape into strands. Flatten the end with the broad end of the dresden tool. You will need to make about twenty-five stamens for each flower. Tape the stamens around the centre. Dust the tips with lemon dust. To create the pollen, moisten the tips and dip into mimosa pollen dust. Allow to dry.

Petals

4 Roll out the white paste using a grooved rolling pin or board. (This is a large flower so don't make the paste too fine.) Using the orchid cutters, cut out five petals of each size, plus an extra five of the largest size.

5 Insert either a 28-gauge or a 26-gauge wire into each petal, depending upon the size. Vein using the amaryllis veiner. Soften the edges and use a large celstick to hollow the centre of each petal from the tip to the base. Dry slightly over a gentle curve.

6 Dust the base of each petal on the back and front with primrose and moss green mixed together.

7 Starting with the smaller petals, tape them evenly around the stamens. Each layer should cover the gaps between the petals of the previous one. Continue until all the petals are taped on.

8 Dust the flowers to give a very gentle pink/plum tinge to the petals, weakening the colour by adding a little cornflour. The five large, back petals should be dusted with holly/ivy and dark green in a broad stripe up the centre of the back.

Buds

9 Tape over an 18-gauge wire with ½-width green

floristry tape and bend a large open hook at one end. Moisten the hook and attach a large cone of white paste. Make a 'cage' (see page 11) with five 26-gauge wires and mark indents on the bud to represent the petals. Pinch a ridge down the centre of each petal using your finger and thumb. To make a larger bud, cut out five petals using a suitable-sized cutter. Vein and soften as before and stick around the smaller bud. Dust with a little plum/pink and again brush with broad stripes of green.

Lily pad

10 Tape over an 18-gauge wire several times with ½-width green tape, leaving the end untaped. Bend a hook in the end and then, using pliers, bend the hook in half to form something that resembles a ski-stick.

11 Roll out some green paste, leaving the centre slightly thicker (this is to hold the wire). Place the paste in the nasturtium veiner with the thicker part

at the centre of the veiner. Squeeze the two sides together and release the paste. You should now have an outline on the paste to cut around to form the shape of the leaf. Cut a V shape out of the leaf, and then soften the edges slightly.

12 Hold the wire in a flame until it turns red hot. Working very quickly, insert the hook into the thicker part of the leaf. The hot wire will melt the sugar and form a good join between the stem and the leaf. Allow to dry for about 12 hours before dusting.

13 Dust the back and edges of the leaf with plum. Dust the upper surface with holly/ivy and dark green from the centre. Glaze using the ½ glaze. Allow to dry, and then, using a scalpel, scratch away some paler veins. If you need the stems to be thicker, use some strips of absorbent kitchen paper, taped over with floristry tape. Dust the stems with some of the dark green and holly/ivy dust.

Waterlily Cake

This cake was designed with a frog fanatic in mind!
The cake top design has been made using the method for 3D découpage.

Materials

23cm (9 inch) heart-shaped
cake
Apricot glaze
1kg (2lb) almond paste (marzipan)
Clear alcohol (kirsch or vodka)
1.5kg (3lb) white sugarpaste
(ready-to-roll icing)
White royal icing
Fine green ribbon
Flower paste
Blue and green lustre colour
Small amount of cocoa butter
Holly/ivy, dark green, black,
pink, plum, cornflower blue and
white petal dust (blossom tint)
Cornflour

Equipment

Sugarpaste smoothers
40cm (13 inch) heart-shaped
cake board
Greaseproof paper (parchment)
piping bag
No. 1 piping tube (tip)
Tiny waterlily and dragonfly
moulds
Scalpel
Scriber
Tiny plain round cutter
Nos. 0, 1 and 2 paintbrushes
Thin cake card
Staysoft flower base

Flowers

1 waterlily and 2 buds (see
page 16)
Waterlily leaves (various sizes)

Preparation

1 Brush the cake with
apricot glaze and cover
with the almond paste. Leave to
dry. Brush the cake with alcohol
and cover with sugarpaste,
using the smoothers to achieve a
good finish. Allow to dry.

2 Cover the board with
sugarpaste and position
the cake on top. Allow to dry.

3 Pipe a fine snail's-trail
around the bottom edge of
the cake using white royal icing
in a paper piping bag fitted with
a no. 1 tube. Position the green
ribbon above.

Side design

4 Roll out some white flower
paste and cut out tiny
dragonflies with the mould.
Paint the body with either the
blue or green lustre colour
mixed with a little clear alcohol,
and then paint some fine veins
on the wings.

5 To make waterlilies, roll out the paste quite thickly and cut out. Paint or dust these with plum and a touch of dark green. The lily pads are cut out, again using white paste, and then painted with plum on the edge and dark green mixed with white petal dust. Attach the flowers and dragonflies to the sides of the cake (I like to lift the dragonflies' tails away from the cake slightly).

Frog

6 Trace the various stages of the frog outline on page 47 on to tracing or greaseproof paper. Roll out some white flower paste very finely. Place the traced design on top of the flower paste and scribe the design on to the paste. (If you find it difficult to see the lines, you might find it clearer if you trace over the pattern on the reverse side of the paper and either scribe or use a sugarpaste smoother to 'iron on' the design, exerting quite a lot of pressure on the paper and paste.) Cut out the various pieces.

7 The design is painted using cocoa butter mixed with small amounts of petal dust. This gives quite a soft effect. To do this, gently melt the cocoa butter on a saucer placed on top of a mug filled with hot water. Mix in the various colours and paint in the details of the design.

8 Once you have painted each layer (I usually only paint the areas that are going to be visible), cut out thick pieces of paste using a tiny round cutter. Place some of these pieces of paste on the first layer, moisten and then stick the next layer on top. Repeat until you have completed the design, and position on top of the cake. Using some cornflower blue petal dust mixed with cornflour, dust the area around the frog.

9 Paint the fishing line on the cake top and some fine lines to represent the water. Make another dragonfly and attach to the top of the cake, just above the frog.

Flowers

10 Cut a piece of cake card to fit on the board along the side of the cake. Stick some staysoft on to the card and, if you wish, cover it with sugarpaste. Stick the card on to the board. Arrange the flowers in the staysoft, gradually adding the leaves. Make three smaller leaves without wires, stick one leaf on to the board and the other two on the cake surface.

Hop

The decorative fruit heads of this climbing plant have been used since the early Middle Ages to clarify, flavour and preserve beer. The plant uses other plants in the hedgerow to cling on to, and it always climbs in a clockwise fashion.

Materials

20, 26, 28 and 30-gauge wires
Creamy-green and mid-green flower paste (see page 6)
Lemon, holly/ivy, dark green, skintone and dark burgundy petal dust (blossom tint)
¼ glaze (see page 6)

Equipment

Blossom cutter (f10)
Leaf texture tool
Medium stephanotis cutter (567)
Hop leaf cutters (600-602)
Scalpel
Hop leaf veiners
Pale green floristry tape

Fruit

1 Cut short lengths of 30-gauge wire and bend a small hook in one end of each. Moisten the hooks and attach a small piece of creamy-green paste.

2 Roll out a small piece of creamy-green paste, leaving the centre slightly thicker. Cut out a blossom (with the thick part of the paste in the centre) and place on a pad. Soften and stretch each section using a bone-end tool. Vein each section using the texture tool, then cup each section.

3 Thread the blossom on to the wire just behind the hook. Moisten and pinch firmly behind the blossom on the thicker part. Repeat this process to form as many layers as you wish (the size varies). The last layer should be slightly smaller, so use the stephanotis cutter for this. Allow to dry.

4 Dust the fruit using a mixture of lemon and holly/ivy. Add a little skintone to the edges and darken in places using dark green.

Leaves

5 The plant has two types of leaf, one that is almost heart-shaped and another that has three to five lobes. They usually grow in pairs down the stem. Roll out the mid-green paste using a grooved rolling pin or board. Cut out the leaves using the hop cutters and insert a 28-gauge or 26-gauge wire.

6 Vein and create serrated edges using a scalpel or by working on the edges with the broad end of a dresden tool. Soften the edges and pinch down the centre of each central vein. Allow to dry slightly.

7 Dust the edges of the leaves with dark burgundy and a little skintone. Dust the centre of the leaf with dark green and then over-dust with holly/ivy. Glaze using a ¼ glaze.

Assembly

8 Tape the fruit into clumps and add a smaller leaf, if needed, at the junction. Tape some smaller leaves on to 20-gauge wire, adding the clumps gradually. Try to tape two leaves at the junction where you add the fruit. The size of the leaves and clumps should increase as you work down the stem. Dust the stems with skintone, burgundy and green petal dust.

Horse Chestnut

The ubiquitous horse chestnut is at its best in autumn, displaying shiny brown conkers in spiky green shells amid yellowing leaves.

Materials

White, cream and pale green flower paste (see page 6)
26-gauge white wires
Cream, lemon, tangerine, dark green, moss, skintone and nutkin petal dust (blossom tint)
¼ glaze and full glaze (see page 6)
20-gauge wires
Clear alcohol (kirsch or vodka)

Equipment

Chestnut leaf cutters
Chestnut leaf veiners
Pale green and brown floristry tape
Round cutter (297)

Leaves

1 Roll out the cream paste using a grooved rolling pin or board, leaving the paste a little thicker than usual. Cut out one large, two medium and two small leaves. Insert a moistened 26-gauge white wire into each leaf. Vein using the chestnut veiners.

2 Using a dresden tool, press and scrape the edge of each leaf, using the broad end, to create a jagged edge.

3 Dust the edge of each leaf with cream, lemon and tangerine petal dust. Using the dark green and then the moss, brush some colour down the centre of each leaf, blending the greens into the edge colours a little. To tone the leaves down, if necessary, add a touch of skintone to the edges. Glaze using

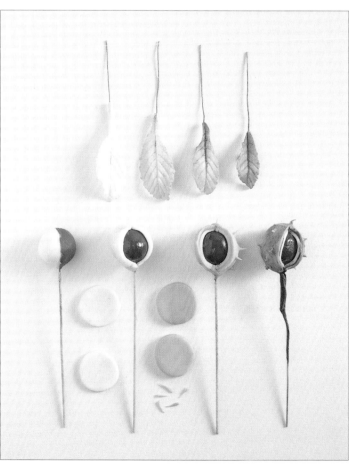

the ¼ glaze and leave to dry. Tape the leaves together using pale green floristry tape.

Conker

4 > Tape over a short piece of 20-gauge wire with brown tape, and bend a large hook at one end. Roll a ball of paste to the required size and attach to the hooked end of the wire. Allow to dry thoroughly.

5 > Paint the surface of the conker using skintone/ nutkin petal dust mixed with a little clear alcohol. Glaze using a full glaze, repeating if needed to give a good gloss. Allow to dry.

6 > To make the shell, roll out some white paste quite thickly and cut out two rounds. Moisten and stick on to the conker, leaving a gap at one side. Trim and neaten the paste to fit. Repeat the process using some green paste, but this time you will probably have to stretch the paste to fit. The edges of the green paste should slightly overlap the edges of white. Working very quickly, pinch into the surface with your finger and thumb to create the spikes. (Finer spikes can be achieved if you roll them separately and then blend them on to the shell using the dresden tool.)

7 > Dust the shell with moss, lemon and tangerine, adding a touch of skintone to the spikes. Mix some skintone dust and alcohol together and, using a fine brush, paint a fine line between the green and white paste (this is to make it look like a slightly decayed surface, giving a more realistic effect).

Twig

8 > Tape over a 20-gauge wire using ½-width brown floristry tape. To thicken the twig, cut strips of kitchen paper and wrap around the wire before taping over the top. Make ridges by twisting some tape back on itself to form strands. Wrap these strands at intervals around the twig. Add leaves and conkers where required as you work along the wire to create a complete twig.

Wild Poppy

There are many species of poppy, making it difficult to work out which one you're copying. This one is based on both the common and the long-headed poppy!

Materials

Poppy and spruce flower paste (see page 6)
28 and 30-gauge white wires
Red, black, cornflower blue, dark green and pearl petal dust (blossom tint)
Fine white lace-making cotton thread (brock 120)

Equipment

Wild poppy petal cutters (547, 548)
Veiner with fan-like veins
Cocktail stick (toothpick)
Fine scissors
Emery board
Fine angled tweezers
Zimbabwean fine fern cutters
Scalpel

Petals

1 Roll out the poppy paste very finely using a grooved board or rolling pin. Cut out two small and two large petals. Insert a moistened 30-gauge wire into half the length of each petal. Vein both sides on a suitable veiner.

2 Frill the edges of each petal using a cocktail stick. (I usually give the flower a little more frill than it actually

has, otherwise the end result can look very stiff.)

3 Cup the centre of each petal slightly using a large celstick. Dry until firm enough to handle (15–30 minutes). Dust the edges with red petal dust, leaving a little of the base colour showing. Using a smaller brush, dust a small triangular patch of black at the base on both sides of each petal.

Stamens

4 Bend a length of 28-gauge wire in half. Take the bend between your finger and thumb and twist to form a small loop. Put to one side.

5 Wrap some lace-making thread around two fingers about 20 times. Remove from your fingers and twist into a figure of eight, and then bend in half to form a smaller loop.

6 Place the prepared wire through the centre and tape over the base of the thread, continuing down the wire. You will probably have enough thread for two poppies, so you can make another looped wire and place it through the other side, tape and then cut the thread in half. Shorten the stamens a little more if needed (it is best to cut the thread on a slight curve).

7 Rub the tips of the stamens on an emery board to give them a little more bulk. Colour the thread in a mixture of black and cornflower blue petal dust. Put to one side and clean your hands.

Ovary

8 Form a small piece of spruce paste into a cone shape and flatten the top. Using a fine pair of angled tweezers, pinch eight ridges on the top, radiating from the centre, and then pinch around the circumference of the top. Part the stamens and you should still be able to see the loop of wire in the centre. Moisten and gently position the ovary on the loop. Dust the ovary with a little green petal dust.

Assembly

9 Tape the two small petals tightly behind the stamens, and then tape the larger petals behind to fill in the gaps. If the flower is still damp, gently move the petals around until you are happy with their position.

Steam the flower gently to glaze (see page 6).

Leaves

10 Roll out some spruce paste using a grooved board or rolling pin. Cut out the leaves using the fern cutters. (These will give you a very fragile leaf, so be gentle with them!)

11 Insert a moistened 28-gauge wire into each leaf. Work on the edges using the broad end of a dresden tool, to make them jagged. Using the fine end of the tool, mark a central vein.

12 Dust with a little dark green and pearl dust (this helps to give the leaf a slightly hairy look!).

Bud and stems

13 The bud is quite small and egg-shaped. Attach a piece of spruce paste to a tape-covered, hooked 24-gauge wire. Mark an indent with a scalpel on either side of the bud. Using fine scissors, make lots of tiny cuts all over the bud to form hairs. Dust with green and a little pearl. Bend the stem slightly with a pair of tweezers.

14 To create the hairy stems, use a fine pair of scissors to make lots of tiny cuts in the floristry tape. Dust with green and pearl.

25

Hawthorn

During late spring the pretty white flowers of this shrub, often known as May, brighten the hedgerows. In the autumn, it is covered in attractive red berries or 'haws'.

Materials

Dark red, creamy-brown and green flower paste (see page 6)
20, 30 and 33-gauge wires
Red, aubergine, nutkin, dark green, holly/ivy, skintone and black petal dust (blossom tint)
Full glaze and ½ glaze (see page 6)

Equipment

Cocktail stick (toothpick)
Tiny calyx cutter (406)
Chrysanthemum leaf veiner/cutters (HH)
Pale green and brown floristry tape
Absorbent kitchen paper

Berries/haws

1 Roll a small ball of red paste. Hollow out a small hole in one side of the paste using a cocktail stick. Roll out the creamy-brown paste quite finely and cut out a tiny calyx shape. Soften slightly and mark a vein on each sepal using the fine end of a dresden tool. Moisten the back of the calyx and position over the hole in the berry, then use the blunt end of the smallest celstick to ease the calyx into the hole. Pinch the tips firmly.

2 Moisten a hooked 33-gauge wire and insert through the centre of the berry, making sure that the hook is hidden and attached firmly to the berry. Using your finger and thumb, roll gently against the sides of the berry to give it a barrel shape.

3 Dust the berry using red and a little aubergine petal dust. Dust the calyx with a small amount of nutkin. Glaze using a full glaze, repeating a couple of times to give a good gloss. Repeat steps 1–3 to make as many berries as required, and leave them to dry.

Leaves

4 Roll out the green paste thinly on a grooved board. Cut out leaves using the chrysanthemum cutters, and insert a moistened 30-gauge wire into each one. Place each leaf back on the cutter/veiner to reinforce the veins. Soften the edges of each leaf, pinch down the central vein and allow to dry a little.

5 Dust the leaves with holly/ivy and a little dark green. You can add some skintone to the edges if you wish. Glaze using the ½ glaze.

Assembly

6 Tape the berries into small groups of two and three using pale green tape, and then join these together to form larger groups. Dust the stems with a little aubergine and green. Tape the leaves into stems of two or three.

7 To form the twig you will need to use 20-gauge wire taped over several times with brown floristry tape. To make a more substantial piece, cut some kitchen paper into strips and wrap tightly around the wire, and then tape over the top. Add the clumps of leaves and berries as you work down the branch. Add some fine thorns using twisted ½-width tape, and form notches by twisting longer pieces of tape and wrapping them tightly around the stem at junctions and wherever else you feel they are needed. Dust the twigs and branch with nutkin and a little black petal dust.

Traveller's-Joy

Also known as 'old man's beard' because of its lovely hairy seed-heads! This plant is a member of the Clematis family and although not as colourful as some of its relatives it is still a wonderful plant.

Materials

Fine white cotton thread
24, 28 and 33-gauge wires
Primrose, lemon, moss, dark green, aubergine, skintone and nutkin petal dust (blossom tint)
Cornflour
Cream and green flower paste (see page 6)
½ glaze (see page 6)
White silk thread
1 egg white, beaten

Equipment

Pale green floristry tape
Emery board
Fuchsia cutter (340)
Leaf texture tool
Fine wire
Simple leaf cutters (225–232)
Clematis montana veiner

Flower

1 Wrap a length of cotton thread around two parted fingers about 15 times. Remove from your fingers and twist the loop to form a figure of eight, then bend in half to form a smaller loop. Thread a 33-gauge wire through the centre, bend over the thread and tape over the base of the thread and down on to the wire using ¼-width floristry tape. Repeat this process on the opposite side of the loop, then cut through the centre to form two sets of stamens. To give the stamens a little body, rub the tips on an emery board. Dust the stamens with a little primrose and lemon mixed with some cornflour. Dust the centre of the stamens pale green.

2 Roll out some cream paste thinly on a Mexican hat board (see page 4 – you need the centre to be a little thicker for support). Cut out petals using the fuchsia cutter. Soften the edges and use the leaf texture tool to vein each of the petals. Curl the petals back using a bone-end tool.

3 Moisten the flower centre and thread the wired stamens through. Pinch firmly behind the flower to secure it. Dust with primrose and moss on the back and tips of the petals.

Buds

4 These are barrel-shaped and very small. Attach the paste to the end of a hooked 33-gauge wire. Using a 'cage' made from four pieces of fine wire (see page 11), indent the buds.

Leaves

5 Roll out the green paste on a grooved board and cut out a selection of different-sized leaves using the simple leaf cutters. The leaves usually grow in groups of three or five, the top leaf tending to be larger. Insert a moistened 28-gauge wire into each leaf and vein using the clematis veiner. Dry slightly.

6 Dust the leaves with a mixture of primrose and moss, add a touch of aubergine to the edges and then darken if needed with dark green. Glaze using the ½ glaze. Tape the leaves together, starting with a large one and gradually decreasing in size.

Seed-heads

7 Wrap some silk thread around two fingers eight times, repeating the method described for the stamens. After attaching a wire to one side of the loop of thread, cut the thread so it is longer than for the stamens, making just one seed-head from one loop. Dust the centre with nutkin petal dust. Moisten the centre and the very tips of the thread with egg white, then twist the thread firmly around the wire. Allow to dry, and then tease the thread open again to give a better shape. Dust with a touch of lemon petal dust.

Assembly

8 Tape over each of the stems with ¼-width green tape. Group the seed-heads and flowers into separate stems of two and three. Tape the leaves and flowers on to a main stem (24-gauge wire), noting that the leaves grow with two sets opposite each other. Dust the stems with aubergine and skintone. Bend the whole piece into the desired shape.

Hogarth Curved Spray

This type of spray is very useful to create height on a cake. It can be wired together to form a formal or a more natural spray.

Flowers

1 short and 2 long hop stems, plus any spare fruit and leaves (see page 21)
3 wild poppies and 2 buds (see page 24)
2 lords and ladies berry stems (see page 7)
2 sets of horse chestnut leaves (see page 22)
3 traveller's-joy stems (see page 27)

Equipment

Pale green floristry tape
Fine pliers
Wire cutters

Wiring

1 Bend the end of each stem to a 45° angle. Tape the

two long hop stems together in an S shape, thereby forming a handle.

2 Tape the largest poppy into the centre to form the focal point. It should be slightly higher than any of the other flowers. Add the remaining two poppies, one on either side of the main poppy, making sure they are spaced a little.

3 Tape in the chestnut leaves, then the lords and ladies berries.

4 Fill in the gaps with the remaining flowers and foliage.

Autumn Glory Cake

The autumn is my favourite season of the year, giving a wonderful collection of rich colours. I've used some of my favourites to create this stunning and dramatic cake.

Materials

15cm (6 inch), 23cm (9 inch) and 30cm (12 inch) round cakes
Apricot glaze
3kg (6lb) almond paste (marzipan)
Poppy and melon paste food colourings
4.5kg (9lb) champagne sugarpaste (ready-to-roll icing)
Clear alcohol (kirsch or vodka)
Royal icing

Equipment

Sugarpaste smoothers
20cm (8 inch), 28cm (11 inch) and 40cm (16 inch) round cake boards
Small plain crimpers
Greaseproof paper (parchment) piping bags
Nos. 0 and 1 piping tubes (tips)
Scriber (optional)
Perspex cake pillars
Two long crystal pillars

Flowers

1 large Hogarth curved spray (see page 29)
1 autumn bouquet

Preparation

1 Brush the cakes with apricot glaze and cover with almond paste. Leave to dry. Add a little poppy colouring to the champagne sugarpaste. Brush the cakes with alcohol and cover with sugarpaste, using the smoothers to achieve a good finish. Allow to dry. Cover the cake boards with sugarpaste and crimp the edge of the paste on each board with crimpers. Transfer the cakes to the boards and allow to dry.

Decoration

2 Colour the royal icing with melon and poppy colours. Pipe a fine snail's-trail along the bottom edge of each cake using the royal icing in a paper piping bag fitted with a no. 1 tube.

3 Either pipe embroidery freehand on to the sides of the cakes, or trace the design on page 46 and scribe it on to the cakes first. Use the no. 0 tube to pipe the design.

4 Assemble the sprays of flowers and position on the cakes using plastic cake picks or cake pillars cut down to a suitable size.

Foxglove

This spectacular plant is one of the most common wild flowers in Britain, recognized by most people at a glance. The flowers are usually pinkish purple, although there are some species that are white or even yellow!

Materials

18, 22, 24, 26 and 30-gauge wires
Pale melon and mid-green flower paste (see page 6)
Lemon, skintone, violet, plum, primrose, white, dark green and holly/ivy petal dust (blossom tint)
Clear alcohol (kirsch or vodka)
Cyclamen paste food colouring
¼ glaze (see page 6)

Equipment

Fine pliers
White and green floristry tape
Cattleya orchid throat cutters (1, 4)
Stephanotis cutters (566-568)
Leaf texture tool
Scalpel
Foxglove leaf veiners

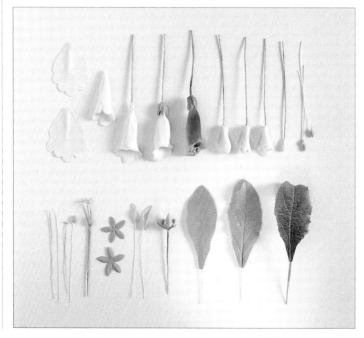

Stamens

1 Cut four short lengths of 30-gauge wire. Bend a small, flat hook on the end of each. Holding the hook halfway along, bend it again to form a T bar. Attach a small sausage of pale melon paste to each hook and dust with lemon and skintone.

2 To make the pistil, cut another short piece of 30-gauge wire and tape over the top half with ¼-width white floristry tape, leaving a little excess tape at the end. Cut this flap into two and then twist each piece between your finger and thumb, until they are quite fine. Dust with plum, leaving the ends much paler.

3 Attach a small cone of green paste to the base of the pistil, to represent the ovary. Tape the four stamens around the pistil, making sure that two of them are slightly longer than the others.

Flower

4 Roll out some melon paste leaving a slightly thicker part towards the centre. Cut out the shape using the cattleya throat cutter. Stretch the two outside scallops slightly and soften all the edges.

5 Using a medium celstick as a support, carefully form the paste into a tube, over-lapping the two edges a little. (You might need to moisten the edge slightly first.) To blend the join, press the paste firmly with your thumb against the celstick. Increase the size of celstick to hollow out the tube a little more. Cup the inside base of the flower. Moisten the base of the stamens and pull the wire through the centre, pinching firmly to secure the flower.

6 Dust the flower with violet and then plum. The inside should be dusted a much paler colour; if needed a patch of white dust can be added. The spots are painted on using cyclamen paste colouring. Dust the top of the flower with a dash of lemon and primrose.

7 To make the calyx, roll out and cut some green paste using the large stephanotis cut-ter. Soften the edges and vein each sepal. Turn the calyx over and mark a central vein on each sepal. Attach to the top of the flower. If you imagine the calyx as a person, stick down the legs first, then the arms and then the head.

Bud

8 Form a ball of pale melon paste into a skittle shape. Cut the large end either side

with a scalpel to form two small petals and then cut the area between these horizontally in two, making the base petal slightly larger. Pinch each petal between your finger and thumb to flatten. Close the petals back together, folding the base petal up last. Add a calyx as described for the flower, using the smaller stephanotis cutter. Make the buds in graduating sizes. To avoid overcolouring, dust these once they are wired on to a stem.

9 For a smaller bud, attach a small cone of green paste to a hooked 30-gauge wire. Indent the bud into four.

Bracts

10 Behind each bud and flower there is a bract. Make these in various sizes, cut-ting each one out freehand with a scalpel, or you can squeeze a small set of simple leaf cutters into the correct shape with pli-ers. Insert a 30-gauge wire, soft-en the edges and mark a centre vein on each.

Leaves

11 Roll out the green paste using a grooved rolling pin or board. Press the back of the foxglove leaf veiner on to the paste to give an outline. Cut around the outline using a scalpel. Insert a 24-gauge or 22-gauge wire, depending on the size of the leaf. Vein the leaf using the foxglove leaf veiners.

12 Using the broad end of the dresden tool, work on the edges to form a gently serrated leaf. Soften the edges and dry over a slight curve.

13 Dust with dark green and holly/ivy petal dust. Glaze using a ¼ glaze. Allow to dry, and then use a scalpel to scrape along the centre vein, revealing the paler base colour. Dust the base of the leaf with plum.

Assembly

14 Start by taping a few small green buds on to an 18-gauge wire, followed by a few bracts. Add single buds with a bract, gradually increasing the size as you work down the stem. When you feel that you've cre-ated enough length with these buds start to add the larger buds, again with a single bract to each. Next add the flowers. Bend the stem and flowers to the required angles.

15 Dust the buds with a little of the flower colour. The smaller buds need a little holly/ivy. Dust the main stems with holly/ivy and dark green.

Fern

These leaves help to soften an arrangement,
and add interest at the same time.

Materials

Pale green flower paste (see page 6)
20, 24, 30 and 33-gauge wires
Moss, dark green, skintone and mother of pearl (optional) petal dust (blossom tint)
¼ glaze (see page 6)

Equipment

Australian fern cutters
Pale green floristry tape

1 Roll out the paste on a fine grooved board. Cut out the fern leaves in various sizes, remembering that they grow in pairs. Insert a 33-gauge or 30-gauge wire, depending on the size of the leaf.

2 Work on the edges of the leaves, using the broad end of a dresden tool to create a feathered effect. Mark centre veins using the fine end of the tool. Pinch down the centre of each leaf.

3 Dust each piece with moss and dark green, with a little skintone on the edges. The backs can be dusted with mother of pearl if you wish. Glaze using a ¼ glaze.

4 Tape a medium fern leaf on to a 24-gauge wire to form the top of the frond, and then add the smaller leaves in pairs just below this. When you feel that the frond needs to be wider, start adding the medium and then the large fern leaves. Bend the main stem to the desired shape.

Foxglove Cake

This cake was designed to celebrate my sister Susan's twenty-first birthday.

Materials

25cm (10 inch) and 30cm (12 inch) teardrop cakes
Apricot glaze
3kg (6lb) almond paste (marzipan)
3.5kg (7lb) sugarpaste (ready-to-roll icing)
Melon, cyclamen and black paste food colourings
Clear alcohol (kirsch or vodka)
Fine green ribbon
Royal icing
Flower paste (see page 6)
Plum, violet, white, lemon, dark green, holly/ivy and primrose petal dust (blossom tint)
Cornflour

Equipment

Sugarpaste smoothers
25cm (10 inch) thin teardrop cake board
40cm (16 inch) oval cake board
Scriber
Small Australian fern cutter
Foxglove stencil
Parchment paper or acetate
Scalpel
Bumble-bee mould (HH)
Tilting perspex stand
Double-sided carpet tape
Green staysoft flower base
Thin card

Flowers

5 foxglove stems (see page 32)
9 fern fronds of various lengths (see page 34)
Extra foxglove leaves

Preparation

1 Brush the cakes with apricot glaze and cover with almond paste. Leave to dry. Colour the sugarpaste with a little melon colouring. Brush the cakes with alcohol and cover with the sugarpaste, using smoothers to achieve a good finish. Allow to dry. Cover the boards with sugarpaste and position the cakes on top.

2 Attach fine green ribbon around the base of each cake, securing with royal icing.

Side design

3 Using a scriber, mark very fine lines on the cake sides as guide lines to help position the small fern leaves.

4 Colour some flower paste with a little melon colouring, and roll it out very finely. Cut out lots of small leaves using the fern cutter. Using the fine end of a dresden tool, mark a centre vein on each leaf. Allow to dry for about 15 minutes.

5 Attach the fern leaves to the cakes using a little royal icing.

Stencil

6 Trace the design from the foxglove illustration on page 46 on to some parchment paper or acetate. Using a sharp scalpel or a heat knife, cut out all the areas in the design.

7 Roll out some more flower paste, place the stencil on the paste and dust the design using the various petal dusts. Remove the stencil and very carefully cut around the design using a scalpel. Allow to dry slightly before fixing to the cake with royal icing. Dust, cut and attach some more flower stems to complete the design.

⟨8⟩ Lighten the lip of each flower with white petal dust mixed with a little clear alcohol, allow to dry and then paint on some spots with a fine paintbrush and cyclamen paste colour. Paint a calyx on to each flower, and larger buds, using some holly/ivy petal dust.

⟨9⟩ Cut out some more small fern leaves, vein, dust and attach to the design.

⟨10⟩ Dust the area around the design with lemon/primrose petal dust mixed with a little cornflour. Be careful not to stain the surrounding area.

Bumble-bee

⟨11⟩ Roll out a tiny piece of flower paste, leaving the centre slightly thicker. Cut out the bee using the cutter. Paint the body with lemon petal dust mixed with clear alcohol. Allow to dry and then paint on some black lines. Colour the tail with a little touch of white petal dust. Attach to the cake.

Assembly

⟨12⟩ Place the tilting stand in the indent of the large teardrop cake. Stick some double-sided carpet tape on its slope and position the smaller cake on top.

⟨13⟩ Stick a large piece of staysoft on a thin card and place on the main board behind the large cake. Arrange the flowers and foliage in the staysoft. Fill any spaces with the extra leaves.

White Bryony

The leaves and trailing tendrils of this plant are attractive enough without the flowers.
They make excellent foliage for filling out an arrangement.

Materials

22, 26, 28 and 30-gauge wires
Pale melon and mid-green flower
paste (see page 6)
Lemon, moss, tangerine, red,
dark green and holly/ivy petal
dust (blossom tint)
¼ glaze (see page 6)

Equipment

White bryony leaf cutters
(603–605)
White bryony leaf veiners
Pale green floristry tape

Berries

1 Blacken the ends of several short lengths of 28-gauge wire by holding the tips in a flame. Roll some melon paste into small balls. Moisten the wires and insert one into each ball, allowing the wire to protrude slightly. Dust in various tones of moss, lemon, tangerine and red.

Leaves

2 Roll out the green paste using a grooved board or rolling pin. Cut out the leaves in various sizes. Insert either a 28-gauge or a 26-gauge wire into the thick part of each leaf, using the thicker wires for the larger leaves. Vein using the bryony veiners.

3 Work on the leaves with a dresden tool to create wavy edges. Soften the edges and dry over a gentle curve.

4 Dust with dark green and holly/ivy petal dust. Glaze with a ¼ glaze.

Assembly

5 Start the stem by making a tendril. Tape over a 30-gauge wire with ⅓-width floristry tape, then wrap it around the handle of a paintbrush to give it a twisted shape. Remove the paintbrush and loosen the tendril slightly. You will need to make quite a lot of these as there seems to be one for almost every leaf.

6 Tape a tendril on to the end of a 22-gauge wire and then add a leaf. Continue down the stem, alternating the leaves and gradually increasing the size. The berries can be added in groups of two and three at the leaf axils.

Honeysuckle

There are many species of honeysuckle, but all of them have an exquisite scent. The plant flowers from June to September and is common to both woodland and hedgerow.

Materials

Fine white stamens
20, 26 and 28-gauge wires
Primrose, lemon, skintone, dark green, moss, plum, apricot and aubergine petal dust (blossom tint)
Pale melon and mid-green flower paste (see page 6)
¼ glaze (see page 6)

Equipment

Pale green floristry tape
Honeysuckle cutters (HS1, 2, 3)
Simple leaf cutters (225–232)
Rose leaf veiner

Stamens

1 Bend three stamens in half to form six. Pull one of the stamens so that it is a little longer than the others (representing the pistil). Tape these to a 26-gauge wire using ¼-width floristry tape.

2 Dust the tips of the five stamens with a mixture of lemon and skintone petal dust. The pistil should be coloured pale moss green.

Flower

3 Roll a small ball of melon paste into a cone, and then pinch out the base between your fingers and thumbs to form a pedestal. Using a celstick, roll out the base of this to make it much finer. Cut out the flower using the required size of cutter.

4 Stretch the four upper petals by rolling them with the celstick. Pick the flower up and, using the pointed end of the tool, open up the centre.

5 Rest the flower on the side of your finger and, using the broad end of a dresden tool, press several times on the central section of the four upper petals to give a slightly hollowed appearance.

6 Moisten the base of the stamens and thread the wire through the centre of the

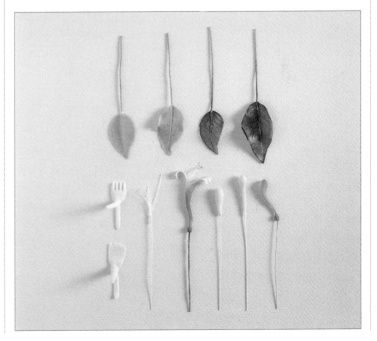

flower. Thin down the back slightly and then bend it gently into a loose S shape. Curl the stamens a little towards the four upper petals. Curl the long petal and the upper ones back.

7 ▷ Each flower has a tiny calyx at the base. This is made by attaching a piece of paste at the base, and then snipping several times with scissors.

Buds

8 ▷ Roll a ball of paste into a cone and insert a moistened 28-gauge wire into the fine end. Thin down the cone between your fingers and thumb, and bend it as for the flower. Attach a calyx. You will need to make lots of buds in various sizes.

Leaves

9 ▷ Roll out some green paste on a grooved board. Cut out the leaves in pairs of various sizes. Insert a moistened 28-gauge wire into the thick ridge. Vein using a rose leaf veiner. Soften the edges and pinch down the centre of each leaf. Bend the leaf a little to give some movement.

10 ▷ Dust the leaves with moss and a little dark green. Glaze with a ¼ glaze. Allow to dry, and then add a touch of plum at the base near the centre vein.

Assembly

11 ▷ Tape the buds in bunches of about ten, taping first the small buds together and then the larger ones. Add a few flowers to each clump. (I prefer to use very few flowers as I think the buds give a much softer feel to the clump.)

12 ▷ Dust the calyces and smaller buds with moss green. Dust the underside and a little of the base on the upper side of each bud with a mixture of lemon and primrose. Colour the upper sides of the buds and the backs of the flowers with apricot, plum and then a touch of aubergine.

13 ▷ Tape two leaves just below each clump of flowers and buds.

14 ▷ To form a long stem, tape the leaves in pairs on to a 20-gauge wire using ½-width tape. Add clumps of small buds first, and then continue with the leaves. Add larger groups of flowers as needed. Dust the stems with plum and moss green.

Wild Rose

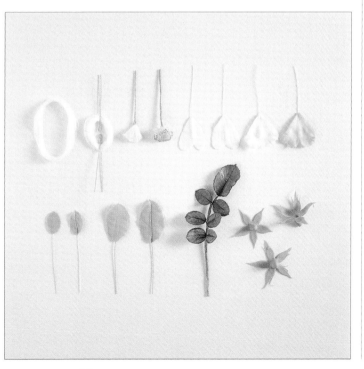

There are many types of wild rose: this one is based on the unfortunately named 'dog' rose. I prefer the sound of its Latin name, Rosa canina. It produces a beautiful flower with a very delicate scent.

Materials

24, 28 and 30-gauge wires
Fine white lace-making cotton thread (brock 120)
1 egg white, beaten
Lemon, primrose, moss, fuchsia, plum, dark green and white petal dust (blossom tint)
Pale melon and mid-holly/ivy flower paste (see page 6)
Cornflour
½ glaze (see page 6)

Equipment

Pale green floristry tape
Emery board
Night-light (optional)
Scriber
Heart cutter (331)
Christmas rose veiner
Calyx cutters (R12, 11)
Rose leaf cutters (B6)
Rose leaf veiner

Stamens

1 Bend a length of 30-gauge wire in half. Hold the bend between your finger and thumb, and twist to form a tiny loop.

2 Wrap some thread around two fingers (slightly parted) about 40 times. Remove from your fingers and twist into a figure of eight, and then bend in half to form a smaller loop.

3 Thread the prepared wire through the centre and tape over the base of the thread down on to the wire. Bend and twist another wire and insert into the opposite side of the loop of thread. Tape in the same way, then cut the thread in two.

4 Trim the thread slightly, and then rub the tips against an emery board to give a little bulk to the stamens. Dip the stamens into egg white, remove the excess moisture using some absorbent kitchen paper, and allow to dry. Dust the stamens with a mixture of lemon and primrose. If you want the flower to look mature, singe

41

the stamen tips using the heat from a night-light. (Be very careful as the thread can easily catch light.) Using a scriber, separate the threads a little.

5 Attach a tiny piece of pale green paste to the loop in the centre of the thread. Dust with a touch of primrose and moss green.

Petals

6 Roll out some pale melon paste very finely on a grooved rolling pin or board. Cut out five heart-shaped petals and insert a moistened 30-gauge wire into the thick ridge of each.

7 Vein each petal using the Christmas rose veiner, and then gently soften the edges by rolling slightly with a cocktail stick. Using a bone end tool, cup the petal twice (once on either side of the wire). Curl back the edges and allow to rest for 5

minutes. Dust the base with a mixture of primrose and corn-flour, and then dust the edges with fuchsia, a little plum and cornflour. The more mature the flower is, the paler it should be.

8 Tape the petals around the stamens, allowing five for each flower, and trying not to overlap the petals evenly.

Calyx

9 Roll out some dark green paste on a Mexican hat board (see page 4), or form a cone and pinch around the base to form the Mexican hat shape, rolling with a celstick or cocktail stick to thin it out. Cut out a calyx shape and elongate each sepal with a celstick. Turn the calyx over and rest on a pad. Cup each sepal using the rounded end of the celstick.

10 Dust the inside of the calyx with white petal dust, moisten and then thread the wired flower through the centre until the calyx fits tightly behind the flower. Make sure that you have a sepal in between each petal. Curl the sepals back and snip the edges with scissors. Dust the calyx with moss and dark green.

Leaves

11 The leaves grow in groups of three, five and seven, with the largest leaf at the top.

12 Roll out some mid-green paste on a grooved board and cut out the leaves with the

rose leaf cutters. Insert a moistened 28-gauge wire into the thick ridge. Vein each leaf and soften the edges gently. Allow to dry a little.

13 Dust the back of each leaf with a mixture of white and dark green. The edge is dusted with a little plum, and then the upper surface is over-dusted with moss and dark green. Glaze using a ½ glaze and leave to dry. Tape the leaves together as shown.

Buds

14 Bend an open hook in the end of a 24-gauge wire. Roll a ball of white paste into a cone shape. Moisten the wire and insert it into the base of the cone, pinching the paste firmly on to the wire at the base. Allow to dry.

15 Roll out some pale melon paste very finely and cut out five petals. Soften the edges and moisten the base of each. Wrap one petal around the wired cone, tucking in one side to form a tight spiral. Make sure the cone is completely hidden.

16 Place a second and then a third petal around the first, sticking down the left-hand side of each petal and gently arranging the right-hand sides over the left-hand sides. Curl back the edges. Add a small calyx as for the flower. To make a larger bud, leave the edges uncurled and add two further petals. Curl the edges back and add a calyx.

Scented Summer Cake

This cake could be used to celebrate a birthday, wedding or anniversary. It is very simple in design, the main decoration being an informal spray of summer flowers.

Materials

20cm (8 inch) oval cake
Apricot glaze
750g (1½ lb) almond paste (marzipan)
Clear alcohol (kirsch or vodka)
1kg (2lb) pale pink sugarpaste (ready-to-roll icing)
Fine willow green ribbon
White and green royal icing
Fuchsia petal dust

Equipment

Sugarpaste smoothers
30cm (12 inch) oval cake board
Plain scallop crimpers
Scriber
Greaseproof paper (parchment) piping bags
2 no. 0 piping tubes (tips)
Cake pick

Flowers

5 white bryony stems (see page 38)
3 wild roses (see page 41)
3 wild rose buds
5 clumps of honeysuckle (see page 39)
Honeysuckle foliage
Rose leaves

Preparation

1 Brush the cake with apricot glaze and cover with almond paste. Allow to dry. Brush the cake with alcohol and cover with sugarpaste, using smoothers to achieve a good finish. Allow to dry. Cover the cake board with sugarpaste and crimp the edge. Place the cake on the board. Attach a fine green ribbon around the base of the cake and position a small bow to one side.

Embroidery

2 Trace the embroidery design on page 46 on to a strip of greaseproof paper. Wrap the paper around the cake and scribe the design on to the cake surface. Remove the paper.

3 Fit two piping bags with no. 0 tubes. Fill one bag with white royal icing and the other with green. Pipe the design on to the cake following the scribed lines.

4 Use the pointed end of a celstick to create the 'eye-holes', and then pipe around them with white icing.

5 Allow the embroidery to dry and then dust areas of the design with a touch of fuchsia pink.

Scented summer spray

6 Wire together the stems of white bryony to form the basic outline of the spray.

7 Add the roses and foliage into the main body of the spray.

8 Fill in the gaps using the honeysuckle and foliage.

9 Position the spray in a cake pick on the cake.

Templates

Scented Summer Cake
(page 43)

Foxglove Cake
(page 35)
stencil design
(kindly supplied by
Marjorie Corrie)

Autumn Glory Cake
(page 30)
side decoration

top

Spring Woodland Cake
(page 13)
brush embroidery
design

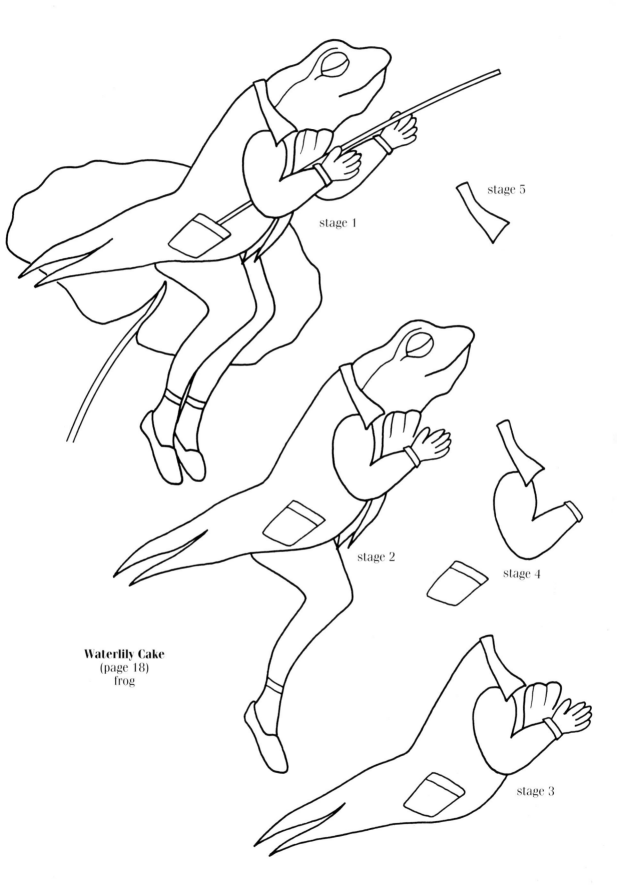

stage 5

stage 1

stage 2

stage 4

Waterlily Cake
(page 18)
frog

stage 3

For further information on products used
within this publication, please contact our
Customer Services team.

Culpitt Limited
Jubilee Industrial Estate
Ashington
Northumberland
NE63 8UQ

Tel 0845 601 0574
customer.services@culpitt.com